After the Rain

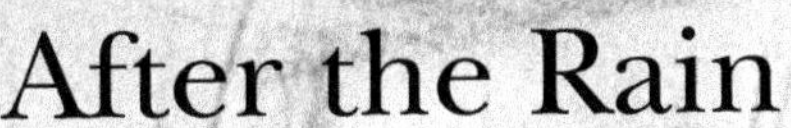

After the Rain

New and Selected Poems
1991 - 2016

George Gunn

Kennedy & Boyd
an imprint of
Zeticula Ltd
Unit 13,
196 Rose Street,
Edinburgh,
EH2 4AT,
Scotland

http://www.kennedyandboyd.co.uk
admin@kennedyandboyd.co.uk

First published 2018:

Title page sketch by George Gunn in homage to Leonardo da Vinci, after whose rain came the less charitable.

ISBN 978-1-84921-171-0

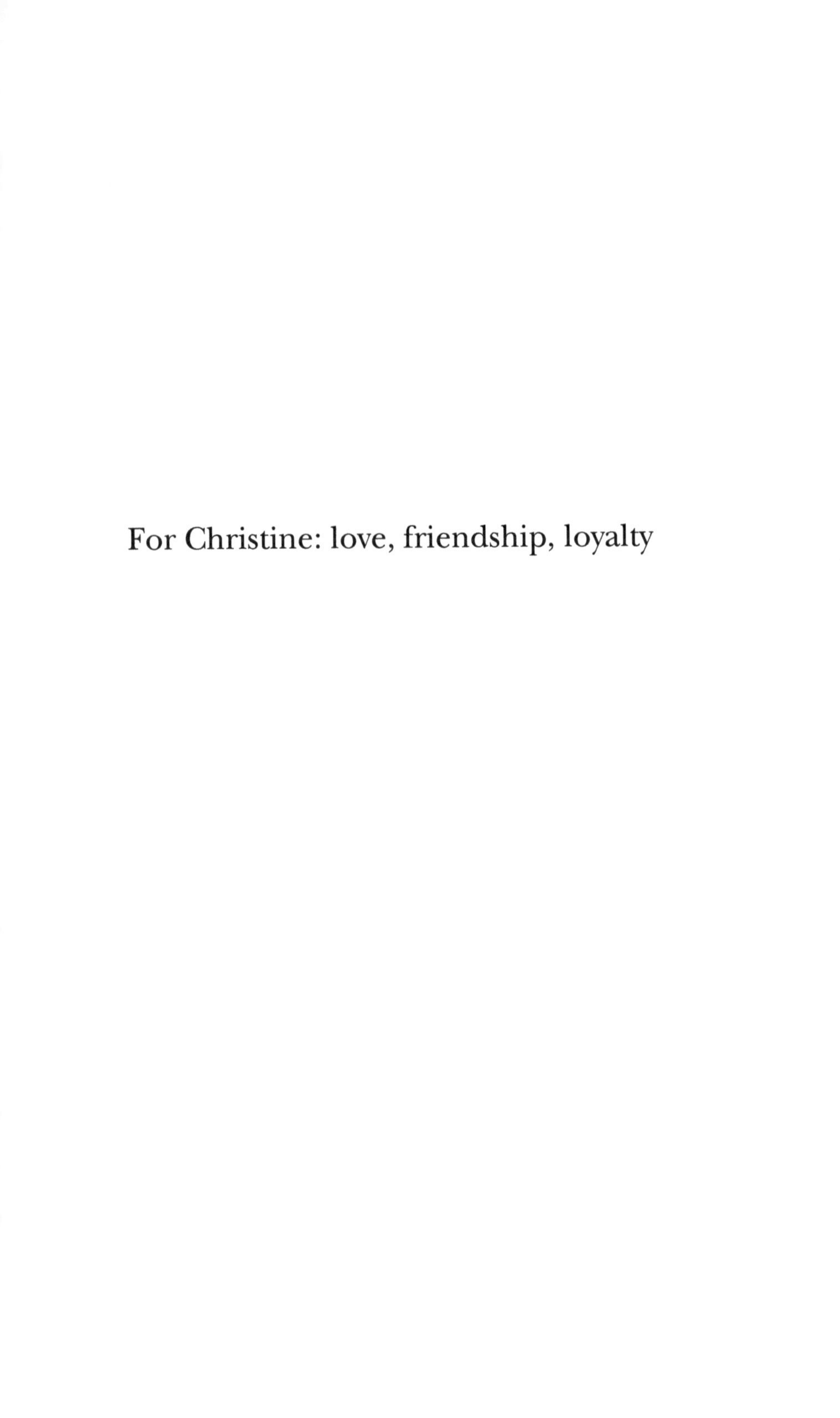

For Christine: love, friendship, loyalty

Acknowledgements

to Chapman, Two Ravens and Braevalla for permission to reprint.

Some of these poems, or versions of them, have appeared in the following places and in various limited editions:

Northwords Now, Pulteney Pressings, The Brough Anthology, Strathnaver Museum Editions, Lus Poetry Press, Islands Book Trust, Homecoming 2009, The Ceilidh Place, New Writing Scotland, The Scottish Review, Bella Caledonia, Moving Times, Neu Reekie, Scotia Nova, Glasgow Review of Books, Distill, The One O'Clock Gun, Northwords Now, The Scotsman, The Herald, Poetry Scotland.

Contents

from Sting, *1991*

On Dwarick Head

The wind is my stinging radiance, the sea
like angry marble jests with cliffs
slapping their sides & then to me
the seagulls screech a shower of "ifs"

if this place, lying like the brown back
of some still-sailing ship
would buckle now & lose its track
what good to me this wind, this grip?

But joy is young & now the Sun breaks through
the rolling prison of the clouds
are we only what we say & do?
If so, then here is only space for crowds

ah village, below me like a ragged cross
you spread yourself between the showers
& Spring above your blue roof bites like moss
& I, here too, chew through my hours

where is panic now, as from field to beach
the North wind knocks our pendulum
& like lightning flashing just out of reach
we sway & crack in our tidy Jerusalem?

Trinity

Sutherland, your name sits on the page
like a ridge of hills
my vast brown angel
how you gave me poetry

Ross, your craggy lyric in my veins
like the song of a cnoc or a scree
you are distance & space
close to the savannah of my tongue

I, Gallaibh, Norse & Celt
Caithness shapes my trinity
my grand linking sisters
your power sends me ranting for justice

your people in my voice like a christening

Gallaibh – Caithness (adj.); person from Caithness

The Fall

(For Helen More)

Your father one day in nineteen-twenty-two
with two barrels upon his shoulder's fold
lost his balance on the quayside
& fell into a herring boat's open hold

& like that gone industry he fell too far
carrying too much, & later
through two cancer-long years he died too soon
Wick now is dull from the ringing absence
          of a cooper

Fat Man on a Bicycle

It was one of those fine bright mornings
that only June can bring
to the Far North, & he peddled
through the turned-in village
sniffing the salt-cut air
as it blew in off the sea
thinking his thoughts of peat-banks
& silage, of how the clipping
would go that day & about the beer
as his brow shone like the Moon
from his efforts & the hurried porridge
his breath like kettle steam before the boil
his legs a slow Manx wheel
the Sun caught his promise as he passed

The Queen Mother Drives Through Dunnet 1968

The gouchy bitch now striven small
turns the corner from
one decade to the next
The haunting voices she leaves behind
        form & duplicate

Early morning howling wind through window
ghostly shredded wheat of stuff
small & getting smaller
I, cropped-headed, young & daft

bleary-eyed, red-lipped & ruddy
stared crudely, still & bronze
Her hat, her hat, oh like
a cake universe, so ridiculous

I loved its fabulous presence
& her coat so dead
& strung, the unlovely
metal swish of car, of power

Her Land Rover cavalcade because up here
we are slightly rough
This is not quite grouse
country but we are surely slaves, alas

it rumbles through the little village, glinting & dumb
slumbering & skulking under the
Atlantic sky, our flat parallels
Uncaring she rides past, oh wicked mother

I was mucky shoe'd & far too shy
to whisper, bow & arrowed
a peeping redskin behind
an all-too-Scottish hedge

My arrow was not aimed at you
lady of another time, oh no
but at the Sun
the big egg we hardly saw

for were we not about to pull down France
& lay Chicago low, oh yes
these were itchy times
The splattered moment every year you poured
through here, we did not care
          pale, peat-eyed & rigid-faced

we watched the ugly thump of monarchy
parade its ghastly airs
Unusually succumbed some laughed
& waved, the sea-soft cheeks a mass of doubt

in curious amazement at such a drouth
of meaning, a congregation
of point & gape with faces broad
& elemental, eyes blurred & unknowing

on something strange & mistaken
a visitor from another time
when she cleared Kildonan
& Strathnaver for it was she as sure
          as the Duchess of Sutherland

or the Duke, they plodded down
to coast or hell
& now she smiling
waving back, a gesture from a Rolls Royce
        does not right this diurnal wrong

Mackay & Gunn & Sutherland, place-names
of a people's ghost
hang stubborn on Canadian
Australian, Kiwi, Yank, but we forget

as if this is forgiveness built from Time
but in my heart
I do not forget
for in bliadhna an losgaidh or 1968
        a crime is still a crime

but with a wave & a smile & a fur coat
& a chauffeured life
of castle & wealth
the money'd bric- a-brac of the robbing elite
        she blusters past

I hung my bow & arrow over my back
& walked the starry miles
to Dwarick Head
to listen there to my anger fly

& swoop out, out to the Atlantic
that tearful ocean, I let
my arrow that was more
than mine retrace that ancestral route

but she, unknowing, motored on to Mey
& there in the bay beneath me
fat & redundant, anchored
by Scrabster's smiling side, grinned

the Britannia

bliadhna an losgaidh, the year of the burning

Piper

(For the 167 dead of the Piper "Alpha")

My eyes are rivers of fire
& the dead feed on my chorus
on the smoke of a billowing column
on the applause of the bacon smellers
glad that they have not become
the plastic waft of melted hard hats
drifting over the gentle Summer sea
filled now with the black blood
of engineering & the fragile idolatry
of an unthought taking
        I see human tissue
turn to gas screaming its tune
of dolorous thanks through the twisted
rig legs & derrick girders flicked like pins
at the two-handed dumbshow of finance & metal
& the dead sink in the neutral water
so many dead it is hardly bearable
they are at home now in the place of their origin
they fill my voice with their angry song
they sing
        "Fuck you, mate
fuck you" from under the feature pages
of middle-brow papers
list after list like nineteen sixteen
roughneck & roustabout, crane-op & cook
name after name in numbing insistence
singing
        "Back in Buchan the barley is turning

in Scotland now the Summer is green"
        My eyes see the hush-up shape & begin
from within Texan lawyers' attaché cases
it flies out, like a soul, at press conferences
like an invisible smog it both disappears
        & is seen
paving the way for back-handed pay-offs
taking a loan of misery & grief
losing the place while we all watched
grown men confidently hoping that Red Adair
in his red asbestos longjohns
would ride out from the sunset
rewind the movie & make it OK
        This then the dream world of industrial oil
night after night it gets worse
the hush-up has swollen
to the size of Tehran
they park their Cadillacs in sinister places
& watch the sky burn like a torch
between the broken arms of the flare-off booms
holding the horizon still
for the many camera crews
so that we can all ooh & aah
feeling pity in our armchairs at the TV news
        I, a roughneck, tell you this
from the strange country of disbelief
the dead are always with us
we remember the dead

from Whins, *1996*

Heron

You are grey in your flight
over the Ullie like the geometry
of slate you manage
effortlessly your ancient swing

The river, brown in its frothing laugh
hoots & slaps down Helmsdale
great bird of my imagination
will we ever stop smelling

the smoke & how it too
poured down here that week
of the burnings, blown out to the sea
in an aristocratic choke & how a ship

was lost in it, blind in tragedy's fog
& how she waited until night
& was guided to the shore
by the glowing thatch forge

of five hundred fires, Heron
you will taste the fish again
here in this Autumn, by your
thin fields, your red iron-roofed

cottages, forgotten like prisoners
in a photograph of an old war
& those other dwellings which did not
make it & whose rounded stones

lie in the useless jumble
time gave as its pattern
to the silenced tongue
Heron, the wind blows now

smoke of a different nature
Heron, the sea now has become
too alluring, she matches you
colour for colour, she is washing
the back & the face of this
resplendent little country
but she is raging, she is raging
& the years won't alter her voice

Heron, she will whisper to you
of her endless harvest
that knows no season
or Springtime, she will give to you

the drum code of her percussive reason
she will sing to you, bird of Strath Ullie
great free one of the empty place
she will sing to you & meet your eye
so be calm now, my slate bird
for your wings are at their maximum
stretch & you pull the sky
behind you like a sheet

did your friend the gull not tell you
of the green song of the sea
of the white music of its chorus
did she tell you of the yellow

golden sand & the taste of the salt
waves kiss, oh Heron
she must've done
because you take me to that other place

where the dream's result
is kept in the house of Winter
did she not show to you
how our murdering friend

the stone man, how he still
stands upon his plinth
did she not tell you
the perfect graph of oppression's placing

note it well as you fly
how his back is to the strath
& the many others like it
whose spirits animals graze

on dust & echoes & how
his face faces the sea
where countless Gaels went
to taste the sour whisky of a bad deal

& whose only promise was
that in the big sleep
they pay no rent,
Heron, note it well

Kildonan

Leaving Helmsdale & the grey
mist of the North Sea
winding up Strath Ullie like an adder
the strath of rowan, the strath of juniper berry
hazel, birk & the green fern
as purple-sided as a lyric
strath of my best success
& the yellow dust furnaced
into the teeth of the Crowner & Mormear alike
& the ceilidh mor in the wooden hall
gentle as my love's neck & shoulders
with your blue vein river song
Kildonan, my Ullie, you are as Time's orchard
in the cut of Sutherland

Behind the Blackboard

The chalk squeaked year after year
as fields turned from frost
to potatoes to corn & the crows
cawked a liturgy of dead souls & arithmetic

as somewhere the dream of a meritocracy
grazed like an Aberdeen Angus
& Granny Grind-guts chewed its cud
marched the aisles & spat out "facts

about the Empire" & the dream world
of Canaan we on-loaded as religion
she told us everything was there
for us & Peedie Swanson winced inside

when it was slapped to us that Churchill
who was bad at sums still
became great, a misty look
crawled across her fish-head eyes

& Opportunity like Johnny Onions
appeared briefly in the strange Summer
biked & dangling to make us weep
far as we were from its swinging door

Yesnaby

Beyond you America
behind you Stromness
far from me now
the tides changing on you
as I walk the crowded mile
of Byres Road, you curve
in my mind like a film
I would run over the top of your lip
through the equinoxial Autumn
putting words in the mouths
of fishermen & crofters
you speak to me still
a language of salt & gull & wave
Hoy over my shoulder like an uncle

Shelley's Balls

I hear three voices on the radio who could
put out the fire in old England's gut
with such vowelly stuff it would
take the shine off linoleum, they're in my nut

or around a table, earnest & miked up
to the Elysium circuits
of what-nots & thingamays their ears cup
to their headphones so that they can talk about the
        poets

& Shelley dead one hundred & seventy years
sodden on drowning he tried to drink
the Gulf of Spezia he saw as the tears
flowing from Castlereagh's corporate clink

he & Edward Williams, too young & innocent
the voices would have drowned him now
we are drowning all & all content
to do nothing but go under & allow

& afterwards the radio plays a dose of Mozart
to prove that they jolly well know
all about this thing called "art"
oh show me the way to go

home, Shelley, Partick Thistle are on wings of fire
jaguars of a people's hope
moving forward to a higher
league, can the West of Scotland working class male
        cope?

They & you & me & them
kicking stones on a deserted shore
watching for the storm's truncheon
to pass, timid all of us, to the core

for we could not be more dead than now
on Radio 3 on a Wednesday night
a set of voices giving jaw
about collective will & the individual right

on White Street the UDA & UVF are fighting
          amongst themselves
self-contained the Protestants, think I
some men got stabbed, it rained
Shelley, tell them about the necessity of atheism,
          then fly

I speak back to the radio voice inside my head
I say "His song has not gone, it's on my lip
but we are dead, dead
& T.S. Eliot in a Rangers strip

& the Galway bishop's fucking minds instead!"
"We've got Shelley's balls!"
Paul Foot heard some Oxford bred
rowing oafs yell as they ran back to their halls

& the statue of beloved Percy Bysshe
a heap of naked stony chips
ah, majestic literature of the English
to be so treated just watch my lips

so falling asleep just like my nation
I switch those counties voices off
& like a dog pissing in the Clyde my education
won't bark or stop, I breathe in the West wind & laugh

Whins

To be spikey & smell of coconut
so bizarre, you will not
let me touch you
like my love you are
an army before the war
upon the side of a hill, waiting
but I have no command for you
nothing inside me save
what you put there
a sea of yellow
in a darkening world

from Winter Barley, *2005*

Rune Stations

To struggle with the parish pump
& put form to its ungainly gurgle
that is a stone cut rune
to carve a space in urban indifference
& pin our lyric proclamations to their door
that is a stone cut rune

to watch the sun sweep over
a flat grey horizon
that is a stone cut rune
to put your mark
on the morning's silence
that is a stone cut rune

to organise those who will always refuse you
& then cry that they only know neglect
that is a stone cut rune
to mint the lead coinage of the dead
& see it spent on accusations
that is a stone cut rune

to feel the days sail by
like a hungry fishing fleet
that is a stone cut rune
to see starlight make golden
the base clay of mediocrity
that is a stone cut rune

to hear a voice in your home
speak the words which are not theirs
that is a stone cut rune
to comply in this ugly mimic
without knowing what you do
that is a stone cut rune

to lift the flagstone of memory
& count the missing fossils
that is a stone cut rune
to wrap your story
in the short mile of newsprint
that is a stone cut rune

to fish for meaning
in the sea of the air
that is a stone cut rune
to do all of this
& still leave room for wonder
that is a stone cut rune

Ode to the Coming Summer

For PB

The coming Summer swims across the North
& breathes a cool May into an eager June
to coax the growth from beneath the earth

so the little heat can come & soon
the barley will green the ochre of the park
& the thrushes trill their grateful tune

in dawnings that shed the need for dark
& swallows can execute their figure eight
gathering up their strength to put the spark

of joy back into the fibre of their fate
which is to be the season's crowning glory
nothing is too early, nothing is too late

it is the Summer coming, neither sad nor sorry
giver & builder; this is her story

the sky may be grey but there is no need for tears
like the promise of an open hand
the season is a warning & welcome of fears

which can be nourished across the land
cultivated in kind & hopeful furrows
& turned to warmth as nature planned

for we have no need of the weed of sorrows
the living bloom across the field is spread
& defies the desperate & the doomed to their burrows

to play endless dice with the dead
a game that needs neither sloth nor slurry
for the colour of life is constant red

& Summer has a mind it's time to marry
the blue space for birth; this is your story

a perfect pibrochd from the Pentland Firth
Summer circles the ever-moving shoal of meaning
the days stretch & meld the myrtle of their mirth

from Hoy's high sandstone shelf, leaning
their elbows on Morven's accommodating prow
to the velvet slipper of Kildonan's dreaming

in her hill-locked cradle where now
the acres are aggregated in a computer's bleep
the days caress the wrinkles on the brow

of history which is the subject of Kildonan's sleep
this northern landscape of calm and fury
where action & reaction are twenty feet deep

on the soft nether-bedrock of nitrogen & slurry
sweet Summer music; this is your story

if I were a deer made from rays of light
I would run with you across the hill
& splash through burns from day to night

& never stop my itchy running until
I had come to the high mountains of Kashmir
& break out your bright crayons of creation & fill

the blank pages where blood is white & death is near
& you would melt the metal of that moment's quarrel
& summon the colours of possibility to appear

to take the roaring from the sky & oil from the barrel
& shed the light of plenty that only Summer can
that pibrochd which feeds the inaccessible

peaks of aspiration & the straths of our shame
oh, early Summer, put the woman back into the man

make me your messenger & your skaldic tongue
season of laughter & light & love
when youth is broadened & the old grow young

take these sunlit thoughts & throw them above
the cacophony of the pitiless market
& let them sing so that their blood can move

that necessary mountain of passion & thought
& like the breather corn growing in a Caithness field
let them root in the stars to ground what is to what is not

food for only a few so the dead can wield
a steel blanket around the earth
& shut out the light & imprison the yield

of the labours of the Sun - ah, my firth
is the world a seabed to the salt-rose of our worth?

Seeking Angels

The summer footballers whistles sing
across the atomic town
Mrs Cowie measures the rainfall
in disappearing centimetres
& behind the willow tree the midnight moth
flutters silent & white
unaware of time & title
from this the headland is but a mythology away

They climbed a hillag, looked back
the peat banks spread out
like brown green terraces
humanity had cut a cart track to somewhere

From her work she looked up
& saw them
beside her a man with a tusker
carried on
the two boys scuttled back & forth
scaling
above them
they sky was an ochre revolution
the dubh lochs held the sky
in an anchorage of wool
there is a cairn upon the hillag
beside it she weeps
behind the intangible comfort of distance
the sun goes down
he buries his spades
under clods of turf
the family leaves
the hill is empty
except for expectation

They come off the headland
get into their metallic French guitar
of a car
& drive back through the crofts
to the nuclear town
to the rain
seeking angels
in the strange game of creosote
corner kicks
& history

Visions in the Dark

Out there is Sutherland
& over its black shoulder
is Caithness
keeking like a ghost

she strokes his head
as erotic as adding
I do not know their destination
these train bound strangers

no one invites the next minute of oxygen
it arrives like a lung
involved & vital
& everything has changed

2

No one knew how my great grandfather made his
money
but like white teeth rumour does not travel

Scrabster harbour is not a denture set
& Ormlie Lodge no orthodontist's cap

& yet his mason's image persists
with my great grandmother sitting in the garden

beside a beehive & a dead ringer for Queen Victoria
her bun the black absolute arithmetic of death

such was hair & morality in the late nineteenth
century
& as angry as a swarm of bailiffs life went on

3

Geordie Crowden waddles towards his creels
& the existential Presbyterian revolution

like a fat penguin on roller skates
the pier jutting out into the sea like a stone pulpit

& his eyes like two corrugated tin roof sheets
& the wet piss stain of a careless insurrection

spreading across his gowl like a tide
as he turns the key in the bothy door

which opens onto a Sunday of beaches, fields & cliffs
& the memory of a mason who bred a farmer who
        bred a crofter

4

Across the bay, cupped like petals
in the hand of a new dead Egyptian
words drift like smoke
from the distant Winter bonfires

flickering over Dunnet Bay like iced butterflies
coated in peat
they follow no course
& obey no laws other than that of essence

my great-grandmother shook her head
because some bee had annoyed her
& two straths full of people
& a fleet of transport boats

fell out of her harvest-stacked hair

5

The train moves on, ploughing into the northern night
as if furrowing a field of hours to make ready for
        memory

the people are stilled, like seeds in a lofted sack
tied at the neck by the umbilical cord of railtrack
        & boredom

my father said you looked at this Caithness Victoria
& wet your breeks if like a bee you gave offence

so now the gradual assimilation of ages has begun
& years gather in hundreds like sheaves of winter
        barley

you cannot count back in Caithness
you cannot count forward in Sutherland

for the ghosts are still keeking
urging everything onwards

to anchor on the god-rocks
of churchyards, bones, masons, beehives

The King of the Herring

I should be dancing
I dream of flying
through the spicy
itchy air of medieval bird wings
& I would love to stick
the stars upon the firmament
which is everlasting
as blue-tack
but I am busy here as a refugee
down on the ground
while wars are raging
in heaven
I search in the sea-loch
for the king of the herring

Caithness

If I could run headless through the barley fields
I would swim the green tide of land
to Watten, say, or maybe Bower
in the flat converted boglands
where our generations found their form

I would run headless then from steading
to steading, from barn to barn
star bright in the stables & milking sheds
my headless head full of the smells of growth
& silage, ah sweet temptress life

you have strew the stone anvils
of our northern tapestry with many gods
on our tongues sit Thor & Odin
behind our eyes bleed Christ & Columba
not often as the planet spins

will the darkness glitter like this

The Coast of Widows

A broken necklace of crofts
strewn across the sandstone floor
of the north Caithness coast
these sea-beat parishes where the fields
are sea-tang & the hay has herring-dream
in root & stalk
this is where Scotland stops & starts
here faces turn to check the Pentland Firth's
anxious coupling of North Sea
to Atlantic Ocean
the incessant urgency of tide upon tide
& these same faces when the night
opens her black windows to them
look up to see the infinite cod roe

of the stars above

In Thurso One Night

They slip under the eiderdowns of their bodies
the young boys in the bar
resisting their fears & talking about Rangers

when they could be blessed by the soft salt dew
I feel in my hair
this morning as I walk out

to the firth, "Be strong & then be gentle"
I wanted to cry out to them
"like those warriors when your country

was young, men who drew their women
to them as lovingly as sheaves of corn
& only put steel through hatred

don't waste your hearts on the tired
organizations of boredom"
that I didn't is part of my general failure

then the night shut like a windblown door
& Thurso seemed
to slide beneath the waves

a Caithness Atlantis
where love comes
from stones

from The Atlantic Forest, *2008*

The Solution
(For PB)

We walked into a valkyrie of rain
'iceodrops' you said
we were washed in a May shower
of sandstone light
into the egg-yolk of dunes
filling our footprints
with the sucking sound of razor fish
& the brine Atlantic sheen
which hung above the village
vinegared our noses with the iodine smell
of a hay-turner & tractor oil
bread & India rubber tyres
so fat & chevroned
they patterned the black earth
of the croft parks like peat-cut braid
the beach before us beckoning
the tongue of the tide licking at the bay
like an April calf at an empty milk pail
we walked wet to the widening sky
beneath our feet the littered shells
lay random & unsettled like ideas
filleting our tiny fears
of the somehow absent presence of death
we walked weaving ourselves into meaning
leaving behind like a faint rainbow
our promise to the sea-lit sand
to never become a symptom
of the problem we mean to solve

My Grandfather Ogun

(The Blacksmith)

Tall, leaning forward like a pine in the wind
he strode to the smiddy
smoke streaming from his pipe like an engine
all day he worked thinking

At night as he lay beneath the Caithness sky
he stretched out like the Strath of Kildonan
his dream a cradle of fire
his hands constantly searching
for hammer tongs & cutting torch
he formed the earth
with the skill of a blacksmith
he butchered his own meat
with tender metal feathers
as sharp as adder fangs

His smiddy was a tool-stacked temple
tins of washers and drill bits
lathes welding gear & vices
all set in a pattern
to engineer his impulse
on the altar of the anvil
before the fertile forge of his creation

When he awoke the fire was fresh
with flickering orange music
as when rebellion turns into revolution
he will dress in black
with a red scarf around his neck
he will caress the bellows into thunder

but will still hold the lamb
an iron bracelet on his wrist

My grandfather Ogun raises his arm
& the birds of liberty fly around his hammer
his northern smiddy is full now
with the dancing blacksmith's noise
of peace, sweat & struggle

The Breath of Loki
For RAJ

The sky is emptying itself
the horizon pushes up
to absorb the coming cold
for a week it has rained
& now the river's heart is full
the sea off the coastline is brown
ships like ages pass through blood
& memory is the coming ice
driven south by Loki's breath
across the unbelieving ocean
perhaps we will be changed forever
& will never notice that 'perhaps'
that the time has already iced over
in the triumph of the joking hungry god

for like Sappho & Catullus
this age has no biography
only fragments of verse
to tell of what it was
to cut into the stone heart of the state
its epitaph

2

The clouds do not go empty to their grave
they do not die but drift
like living ghosts across the sky
to life's beginning & the perfection
of their own work
where old is new & boundaries & limits
are transgressed continually
their destruction is their source

& so beginning close up again
in this vast Caithness sky
& the time is coming like the storm
when all that has risen up
over & through the hopes of generations
will lie like straw on a Winter field

Those who have been so deceived
tell of their aspirations
in the semaphore of the rain
& those who reinterpret them
sign arrogance as their name
on the underbelly of the cloud

3

The ground is divided between the few
who the many have to pay
in order for the few to maintain their scorn
who lacking the vision of even a forecast
cannot see how it soon will be
for them as the tide rises
& threatens to drown
their subsidy, their privilege, their riches
which they would increase
if they only could
Time will not say
when they can expect the levelling sea
it only sings "I have to do it & I will"
then did

The circling Atlantic sends down
the swirling darkness of her trickster's art
the moment awaits itself
above where the tide's touch

is mere illusion
when the old return to youth

4

So it comes, the grey blue sea
is torn to towering ribbons
as the north wind cuts hard
into the squat sea-facing town
Out beyond the headland
a volcano of angry promise
threatens the firth the cliffs the fields
the breath of Loki has blown
& the beach is gone where once Hector stood
waiting for a different storm
The voices of the dead howl onto the shore
from the raging boiling sea
from the place destruction forged
the familiar design of fear

So it comes, the hard concentrating imagination
snapping like midnight frost beside the river
she will walk there the one whose face
has witnessed what it has worn
no shield can protect her now
everything is exposed

5

Still sleeps the snow
like the secret in a shell put to the ear
the ghostly sound of the sea
will shake its hair
like a waking girl
caught up in the dream tangle
of the awkward driven surf

& put ice in the grey blanket
which covers her shoulders
as she shapes herself into the Duncansby Stacks
guarding the ground for seabirds
for it is the morning now
the earth must wait
for the warming furrow of the plough

No one speaks, memory lies under the snow
in the iron gallery of silence
portraits of versions of shadows
hang from the robbing eyes of rooks
In limps Oedipus blind & alone
Antigone gone

6

The Moon lies on her back
she is dragged through the stars
like a shining sledge
by an eager Venus
eventually both are consumed
by the vast black adder of the night
so that night's promise could be no more
hear the hooves of the new centurions
drumming on the skulls
a percussion of a mud tradition
of potatoes, turnips & hayfields
of the Moon in the frozen earth
the snow in tiny revolutions
the light in the sleepless seeds

The night is an orchestra of hands
the Moons an absence of generals
Venus a sorrow of badges

the snow an the anxious knocking
on the closed library door
white adders are singing the anthems of engines

7

Horses chased them down the streets
of broken Warsaw in 1944
or Hatfield in 1984
or here where a small king's vanity
cheapens the landscape of the voice
Soon moss will grow on the monuments
erected to fresh ideas
& this night which feels like the caress
of a blizzard of truncheons
will seem pleasant then
in that time not far off
down the ruined avenues
where shoes are abandoned
beside battered pianos & dropped membership cards

Ice will cover Dunnet Head
Teiresias, our new cartographer
has changed his mind & now charts
glaciers from Holborn to Hoy
paints Pegasus & Bucephalus
in the margins of the new map

8

The blizzard has us tight
grey smoke swirling around towers
Pasternak at Peredelkino cutting wood
for the infernally tricky stove
whiteout & everything vanishes
Caithness Russia the Dunbar Hospital

beneath this Arctic Medusa
this consummate translation turning
the seabed-north of fossils & ditches
into the savage pure poetry
of a beautiful extreme
at home around our throats choking
or searching out memorable phrases
from our sturdy grammar of brochs & geos

What we knew once we have lost now
it forms in snow crystals upon the window
like the skin of an ice leopard
dreamed up by Ovid as he wanders
through the blizzard in search of Odessa
the snow drifts over his footprints again

9

He sat & watched the hailstones fall
the wind ripping itself against the mouth of the cave
he pulled the saga vellum around him
like an Icelandic shawl & laughed
at Loki's attempt to set him here
stormbound on a small island
the storm laughed back
hailstones bouncing like discarded teeth
but laughing still like judges after justice
after the ripping wind
has caught the offending file
& sent it heavenward or into hyperspace
he laughs at fish farms wind turbines bridges
at Diogenes rolling in his barrel

stones stuffed in his mouth
so that the senate can sit & enquire into itself
on how perfect it has become
roasting monkeys on a spit
immortal in the immaculate prose
of a history writing itself in sand

10

The storm has gone
leavings its tendrils in the rock pool of the sky
Loki the mischief-maker squats down
at the Western edge of the sea-grey firth
he washes his hair in the dreaming surf
high above him a falcon swoops
cutting shapes from the snow-salt air
he sits on the headland his task done
all the sacrificial lambs have risen up
the seekers of eternal youth have settled
for the worm-eyed apples of their own
camera-less demise their impossible demands
on the green fields of their lives
Loki grooms his hair with the comb of continents

You who will walk away from the moment
when your mask meets your nerve
may see golden patterns
emerging like gruesome flowers
from the body of the fallen world
All Loki sees is apples

Captain Anon

(In memoriam The Ghillie Mhor
Hamish Henderson 1919-2002
on D-Day 2004)

Is being dead anonymous enough for you
now that the "D-Day Dodgers"
has been reported in the press
to have been written "by soldiers"?
I sit here in Inverness where the music
is traditional Scottish fiddle
I know that without you the Summer
will still be the Summer
but they wouldn't be playing this slow air
It is sixty years since you wrote that song
in reply to Nancy Astor
& the world seems unable to learn
from your struggle for peace
I only know one thing:
we own nothing
can never acquire it
should never aspire to it
What is anything worth
that innocents must die for it?
The east coast of Caithness
lay like a green slate this morning
& all the authorship of the world was there
for you who ran ashore singing
armed with our history
& a thirst for humanity
that nothing would relieve
I will walk out with you tonight
into the applause of silence

The Atlantic Forest

A boy stands on a headland
& looks at the islands to the north
the cliffs below him drop into the Pentland Firth
to his left there is the yellow sweep of a bay
beyond that a green coast
out way out beyond all that
is the Atlantic forest
he cannot see it because it is a wide ocean
because it is a big dream inside his small head
there on a sandstone pinnacle
on Scotland's northern coast
because he has been told
he cannot see
but he can see it fine
he can see the timber shore
somewhere in Brazil or Nicaragua
he can see a boy lounging in a tree
looking back

Coda

In Caledon the bards shaped their songs
from an alphabet of trees
now a cauldron of storms
shapes our coasts with the revenge of carbon
which lay in bogs for millennia
roofed the people against Winter
& was burned to ensure the rule of law
that arrogant set of prejudices
which wipes its rank across the map
from the Uists to New Orleans
but carbon is the still centre of the Atlantic lung
razing hotels & casinos as it throws the dollar
into the high branches of decline
when the last leaf falls a new forest grows

from A Northerly Land *2013*

A Walk in Strathnaver

(In Memoriam Rob Donn Mackay 1714 – 1778)

"I was born in Winter
among the lowering mountains
& my first sight of the world
snow & wind about my ears
since I grew up looking upon
a land of ice a northerly land
I declined early
& my veins chilled"

Rob Donn Mackay 1771
from a translation by Ian Grimble

1

Too much time since you grazed your beasts
on the high Sal pastures
to carve out an elegy for you Rob Donn
with Beinn Hòb on my left
& the Moon on my right I look down
from Torran Chodal[1] to Strathnaver
on the last day of September
when the wild geese fly

2

Eagles soar above the hill of sleeping
wild geese arrowhead across the sky
west from the sunset over the dorsal of Beinn Laghail
east to Strathnaver & the shadowing river
the surf roars kythe[2] at Torrisdale
the Atlantic pushes the night
like a black & dangerous wave
Rob Donn walks the elegy of sand

3

Now Autumn has come
& where is the harvest?
Who will be on the combine
& who will stack the bales?
Who will make secure
the door against Winter?
When will we see the lights in the Strath
& smell peat-smoke on the air?

4

Samhain[3]

The deer shelter among the trees
the stags roar through the hissing cold
the hind is in the shadows
longing for the open hill
the morning is a screaming wind
snow covers the milk-ice mountains
the robin & the blackbird are silent
under the shrinking sunless birches

5

I am asleep & must not be wakened
although wakened I will surely be
when the North wind drives you
hard ashore in Loch Eriboll
I am asleep & must not be wakened
although wakened I will surely be
when who hid the Pretender's gold
runs naked from Cape Wrath to Duncansby[4]

6

There are Mackays in Jamaica
their journey's end the Caribbean
past Faraid Head & Balnakeil
where Kirsty watches shinty
& the men drink Christmas whisky
in the days before the spark was put
to the township of birches
& the plantations needed no peasant masters

7

Pride loves the hollow boast
of the praise poets to ancestral thieves
whose senseless minds embrace debt
& the patterns of fools
as five hundred fires burned
in Kildonan & Strathnaver
as the night lit up orange
& the day filled with a choking smoke

8

I am alone on the hill of sadness
this year when Iain Mac Eachainn[5]
cannot speak to or eat with me
the cattle are anxious on the high pastures of Sal
he made them famous in the South
I am hidden like the deer
from the loss of one I loved
speechless & hungry I drove down my memory

9

From Mackay's Kintail to South of Crask
the cattle are thin & the price of bulls poor
who will go to the deer & the salmon
& who to the Kirk?
Will they see this in Caithness
from behind their atomic dome?
The byre & the palace merge
beside the promise of the hazel tree

10

In Farr Bay the sea dances with light & itself
remembering the great Summer
& the day on the mountain
drawing out the tone in the sand
or delving beneath the beach for apples
for the whole song not just one verse
on Dunnet Head the Western wind
blows around the root of that ancient dun

11

Up with the eagle's nest high over Syre
I looked out from the wordless wind
of three hundred years & saw
a dog fox dart through a splash
of morning light his tail an orange flame
disappeared into the November hill
oh, I said stand fast my red one
our name is on you

12

Am I a Gallaich with a telescope?
I see Rob Donn look South & East
his songs sorn[6] around the horns of his cattle
they fill the fields of corn with sunlight
he follows a crooked road to Eriboll
& the cold patronage of exile
from the rough heights of Strathnaver on the edge of
elegy
he dreams of Gleann Gallaidh lined with fine trees

1 *Torran Chodal*, in Gaelic 'the hill of sleeping'
2 *kythe*, old Scots word meaning 'to make visible'
3 *Samhain* is the Celtic season of Winter beginning on 1st November
4 A ship carrying funds for the Jacobite army sank off North Sutherland Legend has it the gold was hidden and anyone who betrayed where it was would have to run naked
5 Iain Mac Eachainn was Rob Donn's mentor
6 *Gallach* - Scots spelling of Gallaibh, Gaelic for 'person from Caithness'
7 *sorn*, old Scots word meaning 'to move freely but with no fixed destination'

September
(For PD)

When times are good
when there is butter in the dish
& tatties in the pail
& the fish lies fresh & white
on the board by the sink
this is when I see the pattern
in the stone
& the runes hanging
in the West-blown clouds
are all the instruction I need
to hear the birds in the birch trees
to follow the ageless black paths
signalled in the curls of your hair
how you are September & how you dance

Homecoming

The herring drifter skippers used to use
Morven as their guide for home
surfing through the river-jaws
of Wick harbour in the sepia years
before the war to end all wars

We spread our people like a net upon the sea
& haul our history
from where the fish have gone
finding that poverty is the absence of our own
& tyranny better organised than freedom

We see the horizon & sail on
witness a man cut a way for his wife
through the Manitoba snow of eighteen fifty-seven
"What" he asks "are the wages in Caithness now?"
Ohio, Virginia, Alberta, the life

searched for – is it ever found?
"Tell the boys back in Bowermadden
the crop in New Zealand is people!
I have always been making up my mind
to have a look home for a little"

In Otago in eighteen ninety-four
Scotland was as close as the Moon
now the wild geese return to firth & beach
we know our past came too soon
no people for Scotland are out of reach

The Rowan of Life

1

Look how the rowan filters the wind
how her blood-red berries
celebrate themselves as the Sun
is swallowed in the deep Western Atlantic
& tomorrow's history sails closer
on the ship of the night
the rowan tree is nature's truth
turning the peat sanded soil to sugar
it is the life-ash & the world-tree
a connecting conversation of wood & myth
where snake & squirrel & eagle
serve up the creation of the North
to the spinning story-wheel
of human imagination

2

look how the Sea turns red
how she drinks the Sun
as the ocean becomes blood rowan juice
the colour of history
& the deep salt sweetness of struggle
here where little of its taste remains
see how the Moon rises above the rowan
in the orange East of Autumn
& those who search for the stars
find only the dark matter of her leaving
pulling herself away a quarter of an inch a year
the rowan holds the silver signals of her sister
in her leaves & fastens the thin anchors
of hope to this betrayal of gravity

3

look how the Sea follows the Moon
how her waving hair of kelp
conducts the magnetic orchestra of the night
pulsing her love through the surf
up onto the belly of the beach
where everyone walks through their door of
loneliness
the ever-asking Sea asks
who will open the door of possibility
who will release these caged birds
these aspirations locked in dismissal
this Sea this Moon this Sun
is for all & all must taste
the sweet tang of the rowan berry
hear the music which lies beyond history

4

look how nothing really dies
how this prehension creates the self
from the cold & bitter East coast
to the Gulf Stream stroked West
all songs flow from this joy
the transition into the human
though the rowan tree becomes bare & barren
she will grow green again
as will the conscience of those who look
be reborn when they see the need
to toughen the sinews of the heart
& stand up against destruction
yet we must exist survive rejoice
& swim in the fire of the red rowan Sea

5

beneath the cooling Moon the acrobats perform
entertaining children & the angels
who stalked Rilke & Pert
across the carpet of unknown ecstasies
look how the majority sway
like barley in a September storm
see how the piper and the poet
construct democracy for the angel & the child
while the elders pull them down
into the Moonless ditch
where no pleasure or freedom can breathe
or a tumbler's smile be tolerated
who can combat this ruthless energy
save for the great rowan of love

6

look how the piper the poet the angel & the child
pull themselves out of the ditch
see how they use the heat of the morning Sun
to burn everything from the past
which could sit like a toad
on the beautiful construction of their hearts
what can this mean & become
through the trembling leaves of the rowan
where can these actions fall & land
even when the piper crosses the river
& is over the hill wae Jock O Hazeldean
& the poet walks long Northern beaches
where gannets dive between monumental headlands
the angel & the child fashion their freedom

7

look inland beyond the Sea
how the dreamscape of The Flow
floods & nurtures rivers & lochs
as it stores the singing rain of centuries
in its memory of peat & sphagnum moss
stretching horizons far West & South
see how Morven & The Scarabens pen
the open lung of strath & dhu loch
from the Moray Firth & how Assynt & The Minch
wall up its Western wandering
see a small herd of hinds & calves
drinking in the cool Summer relief
of Cnocglass Water leaving their dancers' tracks
on the red sand shores of Loch Caluim

8

this is the half-land where "what" turns into "when"
where impossibilities dissolve into process
the pure open space of the imagination
so as the red deer look out past death
we must also gaze into the actual marvel
of each human life fully lived
who will hear the crying song of life
over the rolling acres of this bogland
which never stays still nor is the same for long
see how the dragonfly dries her wings
like a small bird on a fern stalk
having been hatched into the continual soup
of the air which itself formed
from the same sucking silt of silence

9

look how this huge space is far from empty
see how it holds itself towards itself
in order to let the business of life begin
like the rowan this bogland is a trembling leaf
or like the basking shark in the sunset Sea
it sifts the elements for its own generation
such is the joy of physical transition
here is the overlife of joy's dissent
this is the democracy of mud & microbes
the limitless space contained in an eye
in the fluorescent journeying of plankton
the slow slime sliding of a black slug
the lightness of the human heart
when the underworld moves - moves out into day

10

now all alone the angel stands
as the rowan grows out of the Sea
look how the child takes the piper & the poet
to the place where the dead converse with the living
where the raven & the buzzard circle
to the broch where the black earth still burns berry red
see how around the world the green hills bow down
to the rowan of life & how her many branches
run like rivers of voice through the rough cathedrals
of the North
here is where we bear witness to the creative power
that hastens the blossoming of the dust in the Eastern
dawn
so that silence can give birth to song
& the darkness pass on to light its liberty
all this must rise & fall & sing the dust into life

Two Otters
(for Jean Urquhart)

Two otters swim in Loch Broom
as the Sun sits behind the Summer Isles
all day it has shone bright
into the dark places of hesitation

now as the day ends no-one is hesitating
not those two otters keen on their business
of fish & laughter & existence
nor the people carrying their own light into tomorrow

& just like the otters
our tomorrow will be different
but not impossible & we know
that the light will return

that this sea-loch & these mountains
will be even more beautiful
because we speak to the light
we move towards the Sun

We Are All In This Together
(in memoriam Yannis Ritsos 1909-1990)

A warm wind blows in from Libya
the surf crashes like white china
on the beach at Kommos
it power-surges sending tourists
searching for their cameras & beach-bags

earlier in the day we walked
through the broken wave
of the ruins at Gortes
where the Roman capital stretched
across the Mesara & reached out
to North Africa with her galleys & legions

now olive trees embrace
the fallen imperial columns
much as the wave does
the girls' legs at Kommos

Italian archaeologists dig out
a silted-up theatre
where hymns to victory
were choked on the dialogue of dust

I would take them here
those who burst for glory
I would ask them to speak to the olive trees
about empires and wars
& after two thousand years
the olive trees would say
"We feed the people"

Lighthouses

In Dunnet Kirk they used to put
a light in the steeple window
when a North-Westerly washed
Winter up onto the beach
pulling the sky down
churning the surf in the bay
to a thundering foam

out in the Atlantic entrance
to the Pentland Firth
many a grateful skipper
turned about & kept
his bow into the wind
with that faint light
to his starboard side

across the varnished
Norwegian pine-pews
in the kirk
the Sunday sermon ebbed
like the "Men o Mey"
rolling human concentration
from Dunnet Head to Duncansby
as if it were a tidal boulder
each soul saved itself
as best it could
some lost their teeth
to decades of pandrops
others cut & re-cut a field of hay

men who were ship-fast in their faith
becalmed in such an idle stretch
carved & drew their ships of choice
clippers schooners two-masted brigs
they sail still in the sea-lane of their pew
the deck benches long vacated
their crew all gone the way of light
into the white stone-ship of remembering
built from the arching beams of psalms
for a congregation of skerry & island
a navigation through the firth
of a five-hour Sunday sermon

so we ferry over by the map
of a Hogmanay night
with the Flotta flare-off stack
lighting the low clouds
from its orange burn
while a dozen lighthouse beams
sweep the half-Moon sky
with the ambivalent optimism of radar

we cross from Caithness to Orkney
as the Pentland Firth rises up
& consumes itself
to the West Swona & Stroma
salute each other beneath
the silver cross-swords
of their own lights
carving their names
on the pew of the night
they are the true kirks of the sea
& as we pass
their salt voices sing
of the coming storm

Badbea Revisited

We walked the old road back
from Berriedale to the monument
hugging the top lip of the Grey Coast
zig-zagging around geos
& fractures in the granite
the road inspired & terrified
pock-marked every twenty yards
with the mean grabbing O-rings
of keeper-set snares
the old dispensation cannot let go
human or rabbit
a scream hangs over the sea
here Finn walked from Dunster
a butterfly followed him as he went

omphalos at the edge
centre & periphery
time tradition & torture
over a hundred years
of being tethered to a thankless nation
the people came to Badbea
betrayed by the great liberal conceit
of "agricultural reform" & "market forces"
while Sinclair obsessed in London
about cheviots & the Statistical Account
the dispossessed of the Eastern straths
came to a bleak hillside above a cliff
to construct something from nothing & its cousin
the generosity of the estate

control is the drug of choice
for the sadistic incompetents
who litter the lobby of history
with their ugly shoes
out in the Moray Firth
The Beatrice Field burns its wasting torch
in the distance we can hear
the neurotic hunting hounds
bark their kennet rage
over Langwell & Braemore
the estate has put a tourist panel
at the bottom of the path from the road
it asks in all cynical innocence
"Could you live here?"

at Badbea time stopped in nineteen eleven
all the books written
about the Highland Clearances
sit stacked like layers of sedimentary rock
on some off-shore sea-clett
we marvel at the ordinary names
on the four sides of memory
which at least were leavened with love
unlike the cordite cloud at Waterloo
where young Donald Sutherland fell
where the Highlanders should have bound their
officers
& taken their Brown Bess muskets to join the French

Bolivia

We have the sea
the land & the harvest
so why do we hesitate?
We have the morning light
it shines the furthest
it is never late
the Sun rises red & purple
like a blood orange
over Eriboll & Glen Golly
we must have new eyes to see
the mountains of Bolivia
& the hills of Sutherland
as one landscape for a people free
to breathe in the beauty of a brand new day

In Memory of Doctor Angus Calder
(for Gowan Calder)

I remember when we climbed Ben Gulabin
to put a great soul to rest
& unfurled a banner there
to mark our chief & praise our best
& most loved co-joiner
Gramsci's face high up in Glenshee
an eagle flew from a crag then
to set Hamish Henderson free

at this moment all I see was known to you
your taste was simple
you loved everything
in Orkney the wind is gentle
a grey Summer's day is pulling
itself from island to island
turning the hodden colour of its pulse to blue
you remember this so I can understand

when the simple war of catastrophe ended
you looked at what was left of the world
who could not stop & who could not kill
four black Shetland ponies unbridled & wild
gallop across a green hill
you never claimed a great peace had been born
or that freedom had been truly defended
you wrote the truth & bore the scorn

the skull-hollow buildings along Europe's coast
stare out in disbelief & wonder
& the sea-traffic of memory
is both aid-relief & plunder

& of itself what else can it be
now that memory approaches & fades
gaining in intensity what it has lost
in the private grief of public cheering crowds?

It fades but still stubbornly remains
in the pages of the notebooks that you kept
when you believed in something
a thing so beautiful that it wept
to find itself fading
the Churchill Barriers guard nothing anymore
the block-ships' rust stains
the seal-claimed Scapa shore

a flock of white birds like the souls of the dead
fly over the stone memory of the lives lost
for those who grab & those who release
the useless victory which is the cost
of this present age which knows no peace
only the power of money & its corruption
there was nothing false in anything you said
you were the true heart's welcoming son

you saw all this in the brown smoggy mess
of the autumnal nineteen fifties
when tired men turned to the light
to fashion the future from memories
but memories are far too slight
& about them the future will not care
my love she moves through Deerness
seven red stirks follow her

"What's water but the generated soul"
suggested Yeats to his young republic

likewise we move from fear to the oil field
to reassure where the British state sows panic
so will Scotland force or England yield
who is it that eats Time's cherries by Waulkmill Bay
to watch our culture climb into a hole
to neither champion freedom nor sing of liberty?

At Hakon's round kirk in Orphir
where bulk tankers sit & humans sleep
they will burn the flame of the sagas out
with no examination very long or deep
integrity is a cartoon & art in a pout
the silicon delirium of the age
emptied of fire & topped up with torpor
the blood of nothing on the page

no use to you Doctor Angus Calder
your delirium at least was sincere
a skein of geese flying into the Sun
how ever did our country get to here
where the robbing banksters need no gun
to fleece the people out of their estate
where is the social retribution dear professor
where is the love to heal the hate?

Who will read the rhythm of the world in the waves
or taste it & hammer it out so Scotland is free
of history & compromises & bribes?
This Northern sea will place our poetry
in the ashen mouths of the coming tribes
we will watch it wither salt-dry & die
all the dead poets rise up from their graves
& the sea will hear their cry

I remember when we went to Sanday
an island full of light
the June chorus of the birds
put all our anxieties to flight
Angus it was a chorus of words
that no ignorance can stop or start
all that you knew & felt & loved was in that day
for you carried Scotland in your heart

Doctor Angus Calder away!
I call you away

Volcano

Everything I have ever made
was there a long time before me
will remain well after I am gone
remade by the hands
of those who came out of the ground
& made me & the fulmars
holding the air around them
as close as skin
the molten sandstone
of a low January Sun
returns Dunnet Head
to the desert colour
of its origin
in the morning of the volcano

The Traveller

(For Essie Stewart at 70)

Where do all the roads lead the traveller
if there is no Sun behind the eyes
how can you see the light in the river
if you do not know you are alive?
But you have seen the Kyle of Tongue
in full glory in the morning
you have seen Beinn Laghail grow dark
& above its craggy peaks a warning
but warnings pass
& lessons are learned
& all we travellers go on our way
our life is the freedom of the road
the epic story of another day

New Poems 2016

The Silver Birches of Kildonan

The birches do not stand still & do nothing
they grow & change & are beautiful
there is no stand-off here
only nature wrapping itself around itself
eager within the sap of its own world
which is everything beside the brown river
moving time through their branches
passing the sky across Sutherland
filling the air with the ancient alphabet
of those whose fingers wove the strath
into yellow & green patches
sewn like the ragged flag
the birches fly for memory
as Kildonan shines out of the earth

2

The Sun copper-bottoms the Helmsdale river
with a long scattering of stone coins
an invisible trout or a Gnostic salmon
lip a bubble of supplication up through
the soft silk of the surface water
seeking a fly or a ring or a hazelnut
the silver birches now wear a russet coat
& Beinn Graim Mor is a red mound to the North
a golden souterrain or a broch of clouds
Helios smiths his face-plate onto the April Sun
& the Cheviots & Aberdeen Angus rise
in a molten moment to follow him
across the Kildonan sky to graze
with the shieling builders whose voices stir the trees

3

What how why oh fly
my three black birds of reason
in your cyclical progression
to the managed poverty
then the longed for prosperity
but nothing is constant
save the inconstant dead
so you must fly fly fly
out of Kildonan & the world
for tonight the Moon is full
& sits at the centre of her silver green halo
the rings of her aura fill
the Eastern sky with her translucent face
fly my dark ones across her perfect desert cheek

4

The mist which had hung over the North
had gone & all now was clarity
the river was a brown vein & the trees
a silver & purple chorus no bird
could fathom as the day opened
& Scotland poured in
sensing this the deer grouped together
the ducks thought for a minute on the water
the geese & the teal corresponded
everything became green & yellow
& ancient like the rocks
gouged out & dumped by a glacier
the morning had a story for however
many years it takes to fill the river

The First Lamb

The first lamb is sheltering between two ewes
tucked in behind a flagstone fence
the North-West wind floods overhead
two shochads squeak for joy & swoop
on the hillside above the park
oystercatchers poke their carrot beaks
into the black folds of a new-ploughed acre
a pheasant flaps & squawks from
a drystane dyke in camp terror
half-open daffodils swing like silent yellow bells
between trackside glacial stones

the first lamb is the promise of the Earth
the birth-saliva of belief
lapped from flesh & grain
the thin green grit of youth
the pigment of age in the first lamb's eye
the vast landscape of skerry & geo
a rubric of rib-roast
& bones on the sodden brae
a jawbone drone accompanying
the shochad's[1] comic piobaireachd

the first lamb is the emperor of tiny beginnings
the lord of trembling & apprehension
the brown noise of the dream-swallowing soil
the red sound of being in the heart
in the burn-flood of the moment
beneath this wind
upon this coast
these fields
this lamb
in snow-sapped March

from the lamb's eye weeps lead
molten & burning
then solid
like a rooks gaze
over these headlands
it has looked
heavy & frontal
skirting everything
it flies somewhere else
a chemical vision
a retina of ash

the first lamb is revolving now
like a sheep-headed planet
it is lifted up & burned in the firmament
in the deep blue spaces between ideas
the lamb is an orbital pilgrim
as the sacred sisters of Bethlehem
of Gethsemane of Calvary pass by
the Caithness fields absolve it all
where wolves once roamed
where deer now herd
where ravens roost on overhanging cliffs
in the parklands by the ocean
with the ever-grinding surf

[1] *schochad*, Caithness dialect for 'lapwing'

Prelude

The boor tree grabs the flagstone
it carves the ogham of its loneliness
into the melting air
in Winter it is five adder skins
frozen on an axis of ice
like an antler it ruts the seasons
in Spring it mates with the light
white pleasuring tongues against the green
the boor tree is the Earth's good speech
Summer branches breathe the appetite of music
the wildcat ranges at the root
in Autumn night squeezes itself from the Sambuca
berries
this world will kill & weep on significance
the boor tree searches the long horizon for its kind

Wound

Take this wound that I offer you
keep it close & love it well
for the storm may run at Faraid
the surf turn white Loch Eriboll
but no wind can blow an organised people
across the unknowable ocean
or drown their history in the swell

we are cut & yes we bleed
but we are time & headland & will heal
forging our strength by Naver & Torrisdale
tempering our own steel for our own knife

so drink from this cup
the sea on your lip will tingle
the vast democracy of life

Bees

(An historiosophic ode for Osip Mandelshtam 1891-1938)

Here under the heavy light
is where the poor live
Persephone is their queen
her messenger bees fly
through the nine worlds of Ormlie
where the children play in corners
with i-phones & sugar
they flicker through time quickly
into the genre of silence
with the sea washing around them
idly they paw the floor of their exile
the windows of the houses look inwards
the streets circled like wagons
& somewhere a woman is singing

2

I sympathise with my enemy
for I too know the end of light
Thalassa & Thanatos
the two great waves
no-one will correspond with
or report back from
no eye will attempt to understand
what these bee-borne incantations mean
nervous cryptic confused
suspicious starved deranged
yet the frozen North is beautiful
here people are determined to survive
to be resurrected & triumphant
I smell it on the Spring fields

3

The high tide leaves
seaweed spores
like a form of ancient writing
traced on the sand these words
"Wages are lost profits
& the idea of digital capitalism
an enslaving illusion
a necklace of dead bees
cats chasing balls of pixels
keeping people happy is all that matters
until they are consumed"
Back in the nineteenth century
the present was the distant future
where in the gulag casino the air is free

4

The Spring Sun gears the Voar sky blue
the liminal buildings fold their flag
on this & other wonders
Persephone rises up on Olrig Hill
in a field of newly ploughed ribs
her waxed lips are the Earth's purse
a byke of eager bees
a nervous association of tiny voices
they whisper from beneath the ground
in her language of seeds & roots
about how the sea is green on Dunnet Beach
how the still mouth of Winter is shut
how the gobs of hunger are not
walking in silence through the houses

5

Why is it that
I always move back to you
Persephone of the green fingers
& your black seaweed hair?
You rearrange the air for rain
searching for your mother
like her you exist beneath my skin
my blood is your river
you sift the Sunlit song of the bees
the truth tellers
you are surrounded by them
they fly around your neck like a gentle chain
so that you can always hear the whispering
of the poor man on the Siberian train

6

They plough the quilt-bed of the strath
those who have surrounded the common land
with the flagstone fences of war
Persephone pushes up the dark earth of Time
to lie on top of the furrow
deep & dark like freedom
& those who overcome these fears
are free to endure happiness
like the brief flowers that colour
the edges & corners of this Caithness field
waiting for the bees to roll their golden hoop
from Demeter's barley seeds
the bees kiss the wild song of their yellow language
turning honey into sunlight

Water

(for Alexander Hutchison
20th October 1943 – 22nd November 2015)

"Warmin mahsel
at an aisey fire
A spied blearach on ay waal
ay mease oh ma brither bard"

from Basho (1644 – 1694)

I went back to that terrible
but handy bar on Sauchiehall Street
& it seemed to me that
the same people
were still there when we last met
hung in suspended animation
but not you
even though I can still hear you
telling me about
the Festival International
de Poesía de Granada
in Nicaragua
& the poetry of Ernesto Cardinal
& of revolution

the living this Tuesday are shades
& those who are gone are more alive
it must be this yellow February Sun
exciting the human bees out of the hive
that is Glasgow
you lapped it up in spades
from Managua to Buckie
the lifeline on your hand ran slow
like a seine-netter in the Moray Firth

you took your hat off & said
"Dod, we've aye been lucky!"
It was true, we are the herring children
now you sail through the Firth of the Dead
that is the sum of what we know

out in deep space, Sandy
there is a quasar with
one hundred & twenty million times
more water than our collective seas
are you swimming in it, boy
like you did in Lake Nicaragua
translating local poems into Scots
or having a drink in a dodgy bar
run by the former police chief of Samoza?
We paint our lives like dots
on the maps of our own bodies & annoy
all rulers & their "noblesse oblige"
I bought you a copy of Benjamin's sonnets
& read them to the Northern Star

The Kayaker and the Moon

The orange Moon is born from cloud
mid-February it rises slowly & blooded
over a sparkling six-o-clock Atomic City
unused in its neon-lit Saturday night
to such majestic beauty & casual cosmology
it readies itself in its utilitarian rows
for the usual parade of boy racers & carry outs
the Moon is twelve-inch pepperoni pizza

the day before the Kayaker was washed ashore at Lybster
his battered brightly coloured canoe
preceded him some distance down the coast
he went out into the Winter sea
to perish in the Moray Firth
the coastguard the lifeboat the bottle-nosed dolphins
nothing can redeem us if we are drawn
like light-moths to our own death

the Moon hangs high & silver now
free of cloud & the TV indolence
of a decommissioned suburbia
the Kayaker's safety gear flows
below the Firth in a river of salt
his youth & strength melted into wind & tide
grief is skyped from everywhere
the rising Moon forgives everything

tomorrow the kirks will be scarce of people
but full of the organ music of pushing & pulling
all the ugly conversation washed away
like the sky the world is tinged with regretful smoke
the Moon smothers itself
in the black velvet clouds
beaching on the night like a Minke whale

grief is the hot gravity of loss
at 3.8 centimetres every year
the Moon is leaving the Earth
like the waning shade of the Liberty Tree
it will take its shadow out into the infinity of space
where in the end in the shapeless geometry of facts
everything including the Kayaker drowns
alone in the great mystery of the inevitable

2

The Moon insists that everybody
must draw a map of themselves
on the ripped blue paper of the sea

the Kayaker paddles into his own topography
that is not history or news
this is a breakdown in a hunter's boat

the salt goes into the brain
too little & it causes
an hallucination of water

the sucking fish swim beneath the tide
safe because the shore nets are long gone
rotting wooden stumps tie the beach to the Moon

friendly history sinks wet underfoot
see how existence displaces nothing
& meaning falls out of possession

words tastes touching
lungs drowning in the Moonlight
the Kayaker is sublime in his solitary tragedy

the Firth craves his desire
& swallows his dreams & saliva
turns his skin to mackerel tongues

the Moon pours into his eyes
like torchlight or the soft lava
of new formations & passionate beginnings
now the Kayaker's memories grow like algae
on the edges of the basin Moon
the searchers look in the wrong dimension

such is movement & travel in Moonlight
towards the strange thing that is searched for
the obsession of those who go to sea

they lose themselves in the unknowable subject
of the Moray Firth & the North Sea
adding statistics to their eyes

with drilling rigs production platforms & wind
turbines
& a three million pounds fishing boat
pounding its Polish hull & Danish engineering

life-jackets litter the Caithness foreshore
hard-hats gloves steel toe-cap boots
the Kayaker lies among the sea-ware

the Moon caresses him amid the debris
of the most destructive industry on Earth
she keeps the goats out of the garden

smoothed shards of coloured glass & shells
bleached driftwood & the body-skulls of anemones
a life shipwrecked on the sands of Lybster

Vernal

(In Memorium Derek Walcott 1930 – 2017)

The sea is history
this morning turning
from blue to green
the sky grey

the Sun evaporates
behind Dunnet Head
the hail comes in
cursing over Strathy

the light is equal to the dark
the Voar has begun
opening flowers & eyes
to possibility

these are origins
born to the red-haired boy
on Princes Street who gives
me cheek because he can

he is original because he is
the language of light
on the changing sea
he is fresh like the weather

his darkness is before him
as the sea is behind him
I can hear it crashing
on the smiling beach

in this vast world
we are pebbles
& yet we shine
when the tide moves us

we become colossal then
the boy is legion
unique in his solidarity
tiny & immense
but something is missing
there is light
there is no light
it is absorbed into its other half

the absence of light
is not darkness
it is the picture of the invisible
a map of all we know

space is getting bigger for the boy
& we are hunting for candles
as the energy of darkness pushes
as the light pulls unseen

in the North the Spring is raw
it bloods the cheek
with wind & rain
it colours our tongue

the words seeding the drills
of the open fields
coming to life now
a new elegy

("The Sea Is History" is a poem from *The Star Apple Kingdom* by Derek Walcott, 1979. The poet died on the 17th of March 2017, just before the Spring/Vernal equinox on March 20th)

Nine Worlds

1

The silence left behind by the geese
is drunk by the Pentland Firth
it fills the air with a feathered emptiness

a man looks up from the mouth of a strath
"We get reverse weather in Caithness" he says
as lambs jump their elastic jig

along the coast Scrabster suffers from a schizophrenia
of energy
nuclear waste shipped out in the dead of night
an unmarked ship sailing South to Cumbria

wind turbines shipped in on the morning tide
steel cocoons stacked on the concrete pier
Winter gales painted onto their curved blades

in the Sunlit houses along the shore
phones ring out their voiceless messages
angry ghosts spit on the orange receivers

hypnotised by the pink feet of the greylags as they
pass overhead
the people watch their future heading North
beneath their boots the landscape laments the lack
of geese

2

The savage Spring ice storm
batters the daffodils' yellow bells
& unlike the voices on TV
will not give up
on this rugged ancient country
& moves out horizontally across the bay
lambs shiver in the eighteenth-century fields
& rows of neeps roll like severed heads
in scattered untidy rows
to compensate the ewes for the lack of grass
the sea is the colour of thin green milk
as thirsty as grass & as insatiable as the sea
humans move through Atomic City
like shoals of fish on the flow tide
or stand in dark melancholy
like scarecrows on a moonless night
they tie their lives like flags to a pole
& begin to fray in the relentless wind

3

Poking a stick at nothingness
the ghost of Rob Donn Mackay watches
the bombing of An Garbh Eilean
sees the NATO fighter jets & warships
reduce a piece of Cape Wrath to rubble
he is without cattle or community
& the piobaireachd of his voice
is frozen in the Spring snow on Beinn Laghail
hailstones fall through the mist of his hair
& out of the dust of An Garbh Eilean
Rob Donn forms a poem
& gives it the necessary hard stone music
of the violent age he finds himself in

so that it can be heard as far as Atomic City
where the war workers live in boxes of time

"Soon" he says "on a chosen day
the people will rise up
& fly like the fulmars out
over the clifftops & out
out across the open sea
to the fishing grounds where dreams shoal
in the clear deep landless ocean
& the people will feed yes
fearless & free on sustaining ideas
of their own potential
safe from the predatory lies
of the night-crammed land grabbers
who speak of a good life
in the prison of theft
in the land of illusion & slaughter"

Rob Donn looks West and sings
"The fulmars won't let you sleep
you liars in Atomic City
for your town is full of phantoms
who sell themselves to the cause of war
& shoot black arrows at the stars
to alter everything that has to do with truth"

Rob Donn pokes his bardic stick harder
further into the empty space before him
to trace the shape of the future
& finds the outline of An Garbh Eilean
wounded & shattered
in the blood of the sea
he sighs knowing that we

will kill each other for our shadows
shadows that are milled
to the fine powder of history
as the NATO jets turn to moths
& the submarines to skerries

"The fulmars won't let you sleep
you phantoms in Atomic City
until An Garbh Eilean is remade
standing proud once more in the sea"
Rob Donn is reminded of his own country
in the cattle-filled years
before war left its steel containers
on this Northern shore
before both the wild geese
& the people flew

Rob Donn walks the stone path
until he comes to the stone clock of history
which is accurate once
& for all time

4

Skein after skein of greylags heading North
fly over a hill of skulls
three foreign grey shades
with a hyena on a chain
look skywards but do not see the beauty
only bones & feathers & noise

the last rain of the world
falls on Cnoc nam Fithich
the new Spring Moon endures the night
the shadows move across the hill

the geese continue on
the memory of Icelandic grass on their tongue

night is everywhere
the three grey shades & the hyena
take the low road down to the harbour
& watch a crane load steel asphodels
onto a silent ship

"Remember," said the lead shade
"that Hell & epiphany are the same"

the shades release the hyena who eats the harbour
 lights
& so empowered turns the grey shades
into three fellow hounds
as the ship sails in the darkness to Acheron

a poet who stumbled from a harbour pub
it has been reported
was torn to pieces by a pack of wild dogs

the greylags fly on

5

The shochads have been back a full four weeks now
they have brought us the light from North Africa
& in the Voar everything is a matter of light
it grows like hay in the thirsty fields

the shochads open the heart of Spring with their
 piping
their wings mark an X
on the blue paper of the Dunnet sky

the rhythm of their flight
stays in the demos of the day

music lives in the hearts' core of the shochads
through perpetual movement they become immovable
they are the constant moment of light
a drama of feathers above the rough theatre
of the newly ploughed brown orchestras of the barley
        parks

the Sun so loves the shochads
she leaves the sea naked
to petal-nest their sky dome
a fragrant flight of sea pinks & tulips
all the descent & upsurge of a tide in the air

the birds speak with their wings
as along a road beside a cliff
an old man walks composing speeches from their songs
people will gather like seals to listen on the rocks

6

The coming & going of Sunlight & snow
turns Caithness into a blur
yellow & black butterflies
the size of Stroma
flit across Dunnet Head
the firth is indigo
the streets of Atomic City
smell of the sea
ozone sails across the flagstones
like fog
the dreams of haddock
cod herring mackerel

turn to music
& stick to the boots of the shift-workers
as they board their early buses
& to the stubble
of the growling creel-men
in the doorway of the corner pub
spewing the thick breath of argument
out over the firth
the butterflies love them

history has brought itself this far
& stayed faithful to what it is
so will the birds fall from the sky
& light shine from human fingers?

We die & we live again
the voice at the back of the wind
sings "no fear, no envy, no meanness
& nothing in vain"

This is the sea the land the people
this is the new language
formed from zeppelins of blue lowering clouds
born out of Sunlight fading & snow vanishing
as the night descends with Venus bright
& the Moon a thin cut curve
in the vast dark forge of the North

it is then I see you with your seaweed hair
& your smile like a tide flowing
crossing the causeway from the island
the lighthouse behind you
the seals swimming between the skerries
everything is revealed when you speak

the white birds are flying over the blue navy sea
& I call to you from the lonely deep
as we go now
pressing into the wind

7

Hailstones pummel the eager grass
they harl the skeletons of the birch trees
yellow-eyed primroses at the edges cluster
they have stripped Winter of her thin colour
their scattered passion defies the hail
in the cold air above the low cloud
the mavis finds her measure
she has the taste of the storm in her song

a heron launches from a flagstone ledge
flies out across the naked water
this ancient bird beats back in time
each wing-stroke down a message to memory
the heron's head is bent back like a question mark
hanging over the empty firth
counting out the deeply felt consequences of human
        folly
nothing can be said to add to the wisdom of the
        heron

listen, you who wander the high sandstone cliffs
& the swept essentials of Atlantic beaches
it is not for you to surrender hope
now that the hailstones have awoken this moment
aroused the primrose promise of your lips
unlike the heron you cannot go back
you are the conundrum of your own time
listen as the mavis instructs you

embrace this small storm & the greater storm
that no birdsong can perfume clean
that no paper-boned birch tree can embrace
the salty battered grass is waiting for your footsteps

go now wanderer
to meet the coming passion

8

Our meaning has been eaten away by argument
& Scotland for once has no contention
we have been resolved & like a rock exposed
at high tide are reborn as an island
& yet we have been wounded
we wear a blood-red Summer shirt
our dreams limp to a forgetful place
a province where short shadows fall
on nuclear waste-disposal silos
& nitrogen-swathed lager
cools the hot throats shouting
about empty straths full of wind turbines
where dog-foxes are nailed by their tails to strainer posts
as young girls vomit in the back of four-by-fours
in the long Simmer Dim

the boor tree in the garden has turned
into a flowering organ of mad flutes
a tanker heading East off Hoy
is bilge-full of angry American crayfish
who will put light & meaning
into the green baskets of Spring?

Tell me a hundred times tell me
it is the fulmars who drink the wind

the hissing blue sea on the black & yellow rocks
is the hungry name I call myself
when I am lost in shadows

tell me that the argument has drowned
that the tide will never go out
& that this cold I feel
is the world standing alone in her petticoats
her wound healing

9

The abecedary of the stars
is carved in light & time
above Dunnet Head
with the impossible alphabet
shining down on the specific
anonymity of a self I no longer know
I celebrate & cross the sea
of the heart's desire
forming words out of Death's illusion

the night tells me I no longer know
what I thought I once knew
& that the stars will reveal everything now
they tell me Dunnet Head
is a fallen standing-stone
a runic inscription in the sea
reading itself between the shallow
& sudden North Sea
& the deep & slow Atlantic

these salty Vedas refine my tongue
so I can speak of the stars
& read the night like a book of dreams

so that nothing can be denied
to those who sail to the obvious freedoms
humanity has constructed for itself
a creation nebula both ancient & new
it is the coloured dust of knowledge
forming endless letters in the vocabulary of desire

the rain falls from the furthest star
into the restless sea of syllables
the Sun burns into my eye
the lambs grow warm & eloquent
knowing exactly who made them
clothed in golden words
they dance & skip through the sentences of Sunlight
the rain falls in Andromeda
where millions of Suns conspire to shine

time passes in decades of delirium
& in frightened glances at passing cavalcades
as the heads go down & rise up again
it took a long time but the South is burning
they see & feel it
in the headlines on the TV flashing
in the orders from the light snatchers
which feed down into the marketeers of silence
& the red rusty nail is still driven into the abandoned
gable

in the North we have become radically identical
to the air that surrounds us & breathes us in
as the smoke pours over Beinn Graim
in the Springtime fires of touch & memory
in the uncertain morning hours of reason
that change the step of the running deer

the smoke rolling over The Ord & The Scarabens
paints black the sand in the blocked harbour mouths
that empties the space it instructs us to fill

how can anyone hate the wind?
Even if it blows the flames closer
to the shame of our leaving
with our names scratched on the outside of the window
a signature of oatmeal in the margins
of the printed orthodoxy of flesh
& visions of stones & begattings
beyond the far sandstone mountains
in the depths of the salt-parting sea

a gale blows in suddenly from Faroe
everything is flushed into an invisible corner
the moist coupling of Scottish & Southern Energy
with the Countess of Sutherland
while Death slouches from the Dunbar Hospital
clutching a mobile phone
such is the loyal dictionary of the mind
full of hill-fires owls & cod roe
the last tenderness of the peatlands

Time the actor concludes his performance on Dunnet
        Beach
he buries his contract in the sand
review by review & letter by letter
the North wind feeds liberty to the surf
this is my liquid learning stone
from the cold time to the white war
to this public reckoning of history & words
for in the year of the poet every season is Spring
as the Northern sky tears itself apart over Thurso

After the Rain
(with piano)

In the Summer streets
of the Northern town
the Atomic police
pull the eiderdown
from the sleeping pets
of the dreaming clowns
who search for clues
in the reasonable pain
that ties memory down
in the tedious weather
of the lights going on
in the transport plane
eight million pounds
after the rain

in the season
of the full Moon
different players
of the same old tune
slouch out of retirement
to meet themselves
in the endless losing
they mistake for gain
ripped from the days
that are coming soon
their eyes betray them
in the yellow stain
of a failed discussion
after the rain

the revving engines
of the young men's loins
is the malnutrition
of headless coins
spent by innocent hoodlums
breaking expensive machines
for turning culture into a life-style
no-one can maintain
as the railway lines
sing the midnight fuel
up from the uranium mines
where Abel works for Cain
in the union everyone joins
after the rain

the ship slides in
between the harbour jaws
the drying witches
signal their applause
as the night beams shine
into secret laws
pixelled onto the retinas
of those who look in vain
on the effect that has no cause
to apprehend or ascertain
so the grey wind & the chainsaws
cut true against the grain
of the managed menopause
after the rain

the algorithms
of a bothy cat
wall up the weary
in a fank of debt
where the easy sheep
open a laundromat
& force the Summer Santa
to steam a lion's mane
between the iron price of choice
& the hot cost of that
but Santa's sleigh catches fire
as the reporters explain
outside the museum of tat
after the rain

wisdom & anger
rise up from the sea
seeking a new
simplicity
as the conquered sleep
in an open grave
competing with each other
to look the same
now the wind blows in
through the bare boor tree
at the edge of reason
who can they blame
for this great melee
after the rain

a dolphin swims
into Dunnet Bay
belly in the sand
its life slips away
as the turbines grind
on the bed of the firth
golden wealth
for the King of Spain
the dolphin dies
on a Summer's day
when the gun-runners begin
their new campaign
shipping immigrants from Duncansby
after the rain

inside the Summer
the Winter grows
pollen ices
in the monger's nose
what's born in darkness
never grows
the stalk is short
no weight in the grain
so generations come to blows
in the art of observation
that no-one knows
even as they claim
the revelation of the rose
after the rain

the Lord of Misrule sits down
in his Summer tents
ponders momentarily
the past events
red wine flows
like blood & rents
both transferred to Panama
which he affects to disdain
like the way his wife daily mounts
those four fine horses
the taxman never counts
that adds to his great domain
but the hurricane is coming
after the rain

the hay lies cut
in honeyed waves
the green corn dances
through the salty haze
the Earth gently hums
we all suppose
for it is the glory of our lives
& from it our bodies we sustain
but "I'll be with you whatever"
the mad landlord raves
we hear it on the sea-breeze
again & again
a terror from beyond the waves
after the rain

on a zero-hours contract
the security guard
fondles his piece
in the nuclear yard
his neck muscles twitch
as the loneliness sets in
& he tries his best to restrain
Mrs Mackay from Reay
with her insurgent's bag from Lidl's
that she will not discard
threatening the security of the state
that she harbours in her brain
so he punches her card
after the rain

the closed bells
of the fuchsia
hang like tiny
red amphora
holding fast the risk
of the limits of creation
which no culture
can contain
like the stored honey
of a collected mania
turned into energy
no-one can obtain
down & out in Utopia
after the rain

the dream rose up
before the wind
searched for meaning
in the mind
it is pushed by the dawn
led like a child
behind the Sun
as the Atlantic conscripts
the day's angelic heat
yet it cannot retain
those who eagerly enjoy
the toxic bubbles in the champagne
of the dream's betrayal
after the rain

at last the salmon Summer
journey ends
at the Split Stone
where the road bends
long into the liquid West
there the searchers roam
in the silent glens
as the windmills turn
& the deer complain
of what they see but do not own
they look for a reason
they look in vain
beneath the stone
after the rain

the agraphon

eight million pounds
of a failed discussion
in the union everyone joins
of the managed menopause
outside the museum of tat
for this great melee
shipping immigrants from Duncansby
the revelation of the rose
but the hurricane is coming
a terror from beyond the waves
so he punches her card
down & out in Utopia
of the dreams betrayal
beneath the stone

after the rain
after the rain
after the rain
after the rain

after the rain
after the rain

after the rain

High Ormlie 2016

(for the people of Aleppo)

The Moon is half of an atomic fruit
high in the isotope branches of the night
the peppercorn harvest of the black
star-ground sky turns
the blades of the giant wind turbines
slowly they bowl the strategic
meaning of their being
as up on the hill in the cattle-free fields
the happy slipper-farmer
watches the meter convert
turf into money instead of barley
growing wealth literally out of thin air
& the night cuts deep into December
compressing the light if you are lucky
into a thin paper bale between a blink
of seabirds & the sandstone shoulders
of a changing merging landscape
where the desperate search for energy
their need mapped out
on the boulder-floor of the Pentland Firth
the tide flooding like profit
into the nooks & crannies of a privatized coastline
where driftwood gathers
in the narrow geo where Greed ties his cobble
& Promise sashays back & forth
tickled by the highwater mark
of black liquorice kelp forests
that swing like a pendulum
in the neutered plastic sea
roof-roading over the Moonlit fish-eyes
of tethered turbines sprawled out

like a rum-spree of metal spiders
& Grettir's Mill power grinds on
producing salt & gold & electricity & light
to drown poverty in the Men o' Mey
as the surf drowns grey seal pups
dead now & for all time
like white rotting hold-all's on Dunnet Beach
the heart-broken seal cows bellow
like gut-shot banshees

listen, it is the lost salt voice of the night
shipwrecked on the Pentland Skerries
it is the song of the cut Winter Moon

2

In the Supreme Court the judges argue about
how much fog can be stored in a jar
or whether the perplexing events of democracy
can be agreed upon & called "normal"
as sombre commentators paint significance
onto the bare boards of the dance hall
where Truth waltzes with Reality
moving easily into the realm of abstract expression
often mistaken for music
which is pumped through the streets
of the normal absurdity of Atomic City
as if from an ice-cream van
like raw sewage to the treatment plant
& in the cheap urban bothies
the socially sanctioned stare deeply
into their flat-screen TV's
at the high-definition trivia
of baking & dancing & death
their urban-bothy windows are boarded up

one by one like an advent calendar in reverse
& their manias sleep behind
yellowing chip-board curtains
on mattresses of beer cans & broken glass
& the Moon is still a half wished for thing

3

On the surface of the sea loch
where the silent medium hums
the Committee for Human Improvement meets
inserting substance into rumours
insisting that information is not knowledge
because knowledgeability consists of the capacity
to understand information & its meaning
& to structure it within a direct
perceptual engagement with the environment
no-one perched on High Ormlie qualifies
instead we listen to how Odetta sings
or what Woodie Guthrie sings & speaks
who can hear it now
a voice of inspiration on the flagstone steps
of St Peter's 13th century Kirk
who can understand the words
of freedom that pour out across Traill Street
dancing across Olrig Street
in the morning of elder berries
& the frozen flashes of rowans
& the bleeping lights of mobile phone
& the tragic tongue clacking
of young girls speaking in predictive text
about the human weather out on the site
where they work in dreamless shifts
in identical paper cover-all's
& at night on Ormlie Hill they sleep

in the tightly packed isobars
of someone else's social arrangement
in containers pressed together in rows
like potato drills & the children are barking
in the language of civilization
all sliding as the ground shakes
& everyone dives into the red salt
at the centre of the voice
in the pulse of the dance
& the waiting digital machine
supplied by the Committee
which is identical to their blood
spits out delighted numbers
& from amongst them a wise one says
"Nothing heading our way is modern"
& everybody who is singing and dancing
grows stiff & still
as the morning moves on
down the rough track to the harbour
where a cruise-liner republic ties up
a borderless metal country
endlessly voyaging the tax-free ocean
but anchored now off Atomic City
as white as consumption
beneath Ormlie Hill
where the great Stoor Worm is coiled
where the lie is landlocked
& the truth is far out at sea

4

The sea is normal & green
the sky is normal & grey
a US C-17 transport plane lands
& takes off from Wick John O'Groats airport

each secret month as normal
the MV Parida onloads radioactive waste
at Scrabster & sets sail for Belgium
& catches fire as normal
it is not reported or broadcast
because decommissioning is not normal
everything must go on
& be seen to go on as normal
"Spiritus precipitandus est"
the spirit must be hurried onward
everything must be moved out
past the assimilating energy of the imagination
& everything is failing because it is the way
it has always been so because it is real
because it must be seen to be functioning
even if it is not
because it is accepted because what else is there
except the fake world which is real
as normal which is the alternative
to the green sea & the grey sky
which goes on & on & on & on forever
why doubt anything why ask anything
or think about anything or aspire or dream?
Better to sit astride a lion
while your sometime sister poses
flaunting her endless legs
at the seated smiling dictator
with golden taps & golden everything
everybody & nobody is left behind
the perimeter fence as normal
with a throbbing soundtrack of almost music
signalling everyone into
a place beyond geography
raising a false flag in a phony world

which as usual is normal
as we all take to the air again
as we all get back into the sea
the realization dawns
that everybody has always lied to us
us who are everybody
& the result of this is not
that everybody believes the lies
it is that everybody believes nothing
we who are everybody
cannot make up our minds
we cannot act or think or judge
& everybody can do with us
as they like as they have done as normal
these past sixty rediffusion years
stuck inside the site perimeter fence
on the raised beach where everybody lives

Far out at sea the Stoor Worm rises again
his brown mane flowing down behind his head
longing to return to the ancient high hill
to the Great Orm of Dream
where there is no normal
only the old skald who slouches
through the overgrown planting paths
to the long yellow strand
& the red sandstone cliffs
turning birch leaves into pennies
he spends them in the hungry forest of his life

About the Poet

George Gunn's writing is distinctive, with an urgent sense of people and place. Not 'people' suggesting narrow tribalism, and not 'place' as clichéd parochialism or sterile travelogue. From the off, Caithness and Sutherland provided the literal bedrock of his imagination, and after a writing apprenticeship of more than forty years, his poetry, drama, prose and journalism remain deliberately and passionately rooted in this physical and metaphorical Northerly Land and the people who live on it. To interpret this as a creative limitation would be a misunderstanding of his art and his mission.

A skip though these poems reveals an imagination that roams widely and forages keenly, settling voraciously on a varied menu as it ranges across local, national, international, global and ultimately cosmic 'territory'. Natural beauty, personal relationships, social injustice, political idiocy - fodder aplenty for any poet, and George Gunn's language and imagery invite his reader to enter a world where Thurso and Dunnet co-exist naturally with Jerusalem and Odessa; Strathnaver is no more and no less exotic than Bolivia; Rob Donn Mackay, Loki and Ovid might sit down together for the craic; and relative notions of local, metropolitan or cosmopolitan are truly beside the point.

Of his own work he writes:

"I agree with poet and critic Allen Grossman who argued that, 'Poetry becomes a principle of power invoked by all of us against our vanishing.' Lyric poetry emerged from religious ritual, tribal practice. Every society has a form of lyric poetry. In Scotland its roots are in the songs the bards composed to accompany themselves on the clarsach, which is why I make no distinction between the theatre and poetry. I believe poetry is the language of the theatre, much as Einstein believed that mathematics was the language of the universe.

I believe also that poetry is a form of recognition, a result of observation. The poet stands as witness: not as a passive spectator, but as an active observer – making a reality and a "self" out of the observation. So, observation becomes revelation.

This book represents the edited highlights of twenty-five years of looking. What I have 'revealed' to myself is a society which has changed dramatically in that time. Caithness was always a melding place where cultures met, mixed, came and went. The sea skirts our northern and eastern shores, and the great bog of the Flow Country practically makes the place an island south of Orkney.

What I desire these poems to reveal is not a society remote or cut off from the centre; but a vibrant human landscape, steeped in the past, while reaching out to the future."

For many years George Gunn was artistic director of The Grey Coast Theatre Company [GCTC], a touring company which brought new plays by himself and other Highland writers into theatres, village halls and schools around the country, realising his vision of 'poetry [as] the language of the theatre'. The many professional actors, musicians, community casts, and schoolchildren who have spoken (or sung) his words aloud over the years, as well as the audiences who listened to them in venues from the Traverse in Edinburgh to a tin-roofed factory in Thurso, could testify to the power in performance of Gunn's dramatic lyricism. Since the demise of GCTC, he relies on other companies to broadcast his plays. In 2015 his provocative work, *Three Thousand Trees,* found success on the Edinburgh Festival Fringe. The following year his play *Badbea Waterloo* was given a moved reading at the Tron in Glasgow by the Playwrights Studio, Scotland.

Meantime, he continues to live and work in Caithness, where he is tutor of a new writing group, Ravenskald. In 2013 *Province of the Cat* (Islands Book Trust) was his first venture into non-fiction prose. His first novel, *The Great Edge* (Grace Notes Publishing) made its appearance in 2017.

Quotes from commentaries on George Gunn's poetry

On *Winter Barley*

Introducing Gunn's ... collection, *Whins* (Chapman, 1996), the late Hamish Henderson contrasted him with his namesake, the novelist Neil, another proponent of North and herring.' Whereas Neil's path seems in retrospect increasingly one of a rather misty otherworldly Celtic spirituality, George's is revealed here as representing quite another Celtic tradition - one of gallus hard-headed satirical lyricism. The passion and inventiveness of his poetry recalls the great Pablo Neruda.'

Angus Calder, *Chapman*

'Spare, lean language honed on brittle, sometimes brutal stalks of feeling ... There is a salty, windswept goodness at this collection's "conflicting heart".

Scotland On Sunday

George Gunn is a poet of energy and lyricism. Fearless.

Anne Macleod

On *The Atlantic Forest*

Gunn does what every fine writer must do: he reminds us we are a part of this frail, cold, vicious, beautiful world

John Glenday

'George Gunn has never shied away from risk. His way with words lives somewhere between Dylan Thomas and the Viking Sagas. This latest volume, The Atlantic

Forest, comes rooted in his own native Caithness background, but sails out, as the title suggests, into many landfalls, some real, others mythic. His first line walks into a Valkyrie of rain and many such lyrical flourishes thread through the book. George Gunn's poetry has always sustained a radical questioning outlook ... traversing history, current international conflicts and the state of Scottish theatre.'

Aonghas Macneacail, *The Herald*

On *A Northerly Land*

His many collections of poetry span twenty-five years and have done for Caithness what George Mackay Brown did for Orkney. George Gunn is one of the few poets who can claim to be an authentic Bard of his people. His verse moves effortlessly from the personal to the local to the historical and can embody the national and the international, within the personal, the local and the historical. Few poets can respond in verse so rapidly, and with such vitality and nuance, to "big events" the way Gunn can. In this respect he is a genuine Makar, already proven in the role.

Kevin Williamson, *Bella Caledonia*

Also by George Gunn

Poetry
Sting (1991)
On the Rigs: Images of Life Offshore - *with Photography by Allen Wright* (1995)
Whins (1996)
Winter Barley (2005)
The Atlantic Forest (2008)
Stroma - *with Ali Murray & Photography by Roddie Ritchie* (2011)
A Northerly Land (2013)

Drama
Songs of the Grey Coast & Gold of Kildonan (1992)
Atomic City (2010)
Egil Son of the Night Wolf (2010)

Prose
The Province of the Cat: A Journey to the Radical Heart of the North (2013)
The Great Edge - A Novel (2017)

www.ingramcontent.com/pod-product-compliance
Ingram Content Group UK Ltd.
Pitfield, Milton Keynes, MK11 3LW, UK
UKHW020420250726
13967UKWH00007B/2732